956.04   90-17270
HAR

Harper, Paul

The Arab-Israeli Issue

~~55582~~   51053

DATE DUE	BORROWER'S NAME	H ROOM NUMBER
OCT 1 5 1991	Jeu Mulqueeny	302
JAN 22 '93	LOIDA GONZALO	112
MAY 21 '93	Hava Al-Rafati	106
MAR 23 '94	A. Harureb	108

51053
956.04   90-17270
HAR

Harper, Paul

The Arab-Israeli Issue

~~55582~~

Amman, Jordan 1970. Driven by war from their country, the People's Front for the Liberation of Palestine blew up three airliners.

THE
ARAB~ISRAELI
ISSUE

Paul Harper

ROURKE ENTERPRISES, INC.
Vero Beach, Florida 32964

First published in the United States in 1987 by
Rourke Enterprises, Inc. P.O. Box 3328 Vero Beach, Florida
32964

First published in 1986 by Wayland (Publishers) Ltd
61 Western Road, Hove East Sussex BN3 1JD, England

© Copyright 1986 Wayland (Publishers) Ltd

90-17270

Manufactured by The Bath Press, Avon, England

Library of Congress Cataloging-in-Publication Data
Harper, Paul.
    The Arab–Israeli issue.
    (Flashpoints)
    Bibliography: p.   *51053*
    Includes index.
    Summary: Traces the history of the Arab–Israeli conflict
and discusses prospects for a peaceful solution. Includes a
glossary of terms.
    1. Jewish–Arab relations – Juvenile literature.
[1. Jewish–Arab relations] I. Title   II. Series:
Flashpoints.

DS119.7.H3764   1987   956'.04   86–20259
ISBN 0–86592–029–X

Contents

1
"David and Goliath"

Lebanon, June 1982. Soviet-designed Katyusha rockets being launched by Palestinian guerrillas.

On the evening of June 3, 1982, the Israeli Ambassador in London was shot and seriously wounded by an Arab gunman. Within hours, Israeli planes were bombing Beirut, killing over 200 people. In retaliation, forces of the Palestine Liberation Organization (PLO) based in southern Lebanon fired shells and rockets into northern Israel on June 4 and 5. On June 6, a huge Israeli force that had been massing close to the border for months poured into south Lebanon and headed toward the capital, Beirut, quickly surrounding the major towns and cities along the way. Thousands of civilians were killed, wounded, or made homeless as Israeli forces pounded Lebanon on the land and from the air and sea. Israel's poorly equipped Palestinian adversaries were helpless before this onslaught.

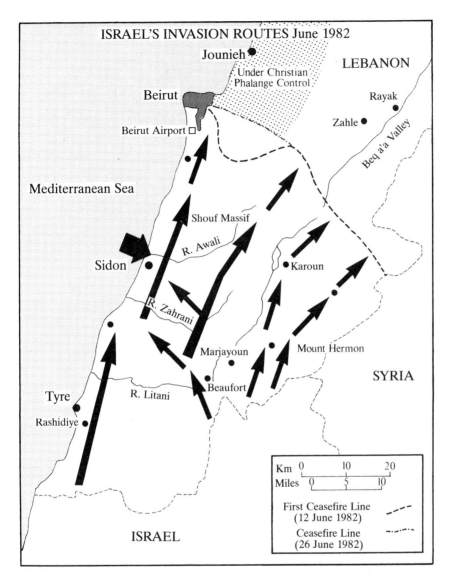

ISRAEL'S INVASION ROUTES June 1982

Jounieh

Under Christian Phalange Control

LEBANON

Beirut

Rayak

Zahle

Beirut Airport

Beq'a'a Valley

Mediterranean Sea

Shouf Massif

R. Awali

Sidon

Karoun

R. Zahrani

Marjayoun

Mount Hermon

SYRIA

Tyre

R. Litani

Beaufort

Rashidiye

Km	0	10	20
Miles	0	5	10

First Ceasefire Line
(12 June 1982)

Ceasefire Line
(26 June 1982)

ISRAEL

The PLO had some 6,000 fighters in the south but against this Israel had sent nine armored divisions with 90,000 troops, supported by the Israeli Navy and one of the world's most powerful air forces. Many guerrillas were killed or captured but some retreated to the PLO's headquarters in West Beirut. This 10 square-mile (26 square-kilometer) enclave was surrounded by Israeli forces on June 10. Its 500,000 inhabitants, mostly Muslim Lebanese people and 8,000 Palestinian guerrillas, stood alone against the massed Israeli Army. Lebanon's closest Arab neighbor, Syria,

This map shows the Israeli advance into Lebanon during June 1982.

9

agreed to a ceasefire after eighty of its fighter planes had been shot down in three days, for the loss of one Israeli plane. No other Arab country dared to provoke a war with Israel by intervening.

Beirut under siege

But the Palestinian fighters, born and bred mostly in the slums and refugee shanty towns of West Beirut, knew every alleyway and back street intimately, and had long prepared a system of underground tunnels for such an event. Urban guerrillas, trained and hardened in the Lebanese civil war, they were determined to make Israel pay a high price for taking Beirut. The Israeli response meant the cost was met instead by the civilians of West Beirut, who for nearly two months were subjected to the worst siege that late-twentieth-century military technology could devise. Thousands of tons of high explosives – weapons supplied for the most part by Israeli's ally the United States – rained down continuously on Beirut. Water, electricity, food, and medical supplies were prevented from reaching the besieged.

Lebanon, June 1982. After launching an attack on Palestinian refugees, Israeli soldiers search Palestinians on the outskirts of Tyre.

By August 12, when the PLO accepted a deal it thought would secure its evacuation with honor, Lebanese government sources estimated that 18,000 people had been killed and 30,000 injured since the start of the invasion; 85 percent of the casualties were civilians. An American-led multinational force was to take over the protection of the Palestinians left behind in West Beirut, which Israel guaranteed not to enter. On September 14, after the PLO guerrillas had left and the international force had unexpectedly been withdrawn, Israel's ally, the new president of Lebanon, Bashir Bemayel, was assassinated. Israeli forces immediately occupied the city. Meanwhile their Lebanese allies, the Christian Phalangist militia, went into the Palestinian camps of Sabra and Chatila, where they massacred 2,000 of the refugees in cold blood.

Beirut, September 1982. One hour before Amin Gemayel (inset) was sworn in as Lebanon's president, a massive explosion destroyed East Beirut, where the inauguration was to have taken place.

11

*West Beirut, 1982.
A Palestinian
woman, at a
memorial service for
the refugees
massacred at Sabra
and Chatilla, angrily
brandishes a helmet
belonging to the
militia force
responsible.*

It took Israel just four days to reach and surround Beirut. Three years later, in 1985, having incurred more casualties than in the 1967 war when it simultaneously defeated the massed armies of three Arab countries, Israel was still seeking a safe exit from Lebanon. Despite heavy losses many Palestinian guerrillas have returned to mount anti-Israeli operations from the south. In addition, a new armed movement – the Shi'ite Muslim guerrillas – has arisen in south Lebanon. Fanatically determined, the Shi'ites threaten suicide attacks on Israel's northern towns, making them as much a problem to Israel's security as the PLO once were.

There is intense bitterness that so many lives have been sacrificed for so little. Why did it happen?

2
The claims to Palestine

The war in Lebanon was the fifth between Arabs and Israelis in less than forty years, the product not of mindless hatred between Arab and Israeli, or between Muslim and Jew, but the result of the failure to resolve the conflict over the land of Palestine, the Holy Land. Many other parties, most directly the Arab countries bordering Palestine, have been drawn into this conflict between two rivals to the same land, both of whom claim it as their rightful inheritance.

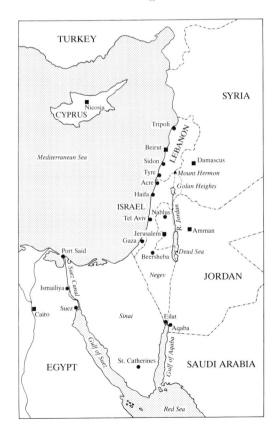

Israel lies on the eastern edge of the Mediterranean Sea, and borders the countries of South-west Asia and northern Africa.

The word Palestine designates the geographical and historical area lying along the eastern shore of the Mediterranean. This area is bounded on the west by the Jordan River, on the north by the mountains of Lebanon and on the south by the deserts of Egypt and Arabia. The 9,000 square miles (23,000 square kilometers) of Palestine consist principally of a fertile coastal plain, separated from the Jordan valley by a range of hills running from north to south. Jerusalem in the principal city.

Whose homeland?

Palestine today is wholly under Jewish control and known as the State of Israel. The struggle of the Israelis, about twenty-five percent of the total world Jewish population, to carve out and hold on to a sovereign, independent state

Arabs have been farming the land in Palestine for hundreds of years, as in this woodcut of the lower Himmon valley.

is one side of the conflict. On the other are the native Arab inhabitants of Palestine, the majority of whom today have been dispersed outside its borders or placed against their will under the rule of Israel. The basis of the Palestinian claim to the land is simple: Palestine is their country, they argue, in the same way that England is the country of the English or France that of the French. They and their ancestors inhabited and cultivated Palestine until they were dispossessed by Israel.

The Jewish claim to Palestine is more complex. On the religious level, Jews believe that God promised Palestine to them for all eternity. The Book of Genesis records that God told Abraham, the father of the Jews: "The whole land

A Jerusalem Coffee Shop, 1920. The Palestinian lifestyle before Zionist rule, was not uncivilized.

15

New York, 1949.
Trucks of food sent
by American Zionists
to support Israel.

of Canaan, where you are now an alien, I will give as an everlasting possession to you and your descendants after you." Historically, Jews claim their emigration to Palestine is a return to what was their homeland 2,000 years ago. Politically, it is claimed that the gathering of Jews in Palestine and their establishment there of an independent state is the only way to liberate them from the persecution they have suffered throughout history as an ethnic minority with no state of their own to protect their lives and interests.

This claim has long since gained wide acceptance in the Western world, without whose support the State of Israel could not have been established, nor have survived until today, in the face of the concerted hostility of the surrounding Arab countries. The claims of the Palestinians, however, have been largely disregarded in the West.

3
Palestine's history

Biblical promises and prophecies were an important factor in engaging Western support for the plan to establish a Jewish state in Palestine. Yet Palestine is the Holy Land of three of the world's major religions – Islam, Judaism and Christianity. For Muslims, the Dome of the Rock, a mosque in Jerusalem, marks the site where the Prophet Muhammad ascended into heaven in A.D. 619. For Jews this same area is the site of their ancient temple, of which today one side remains, the Wailing Wall. For Christians, Jerusalem is where Jesus was crucified and resurrected.

Modern Christianity remains divided over whether the establishment of modern Israel should be understood as the fulfillment of Biblical prophecy. The God of the Old Testament so often appeared to sanction terrible massacres and wholesale destruction in the cause of the Chosen People, yet in the New Testament (which is read and accepted by Christians but not Jews) He is depicted as a God of love. These contradictions have generally been reconciled by taking the Bible stories as a guide to the past and future rather than as literal facts. Most Christians believe that the idea of a Promised Land is to be understood not as the physical movement of one people, the Jews, to one place, Palestine, but as the return of sinners everywhere, of whatever creed or race, to the kingdom of God.

A religious or political struggle?
Although God promised Palestine to the descendants of Abraham, the Jews and the Arabs both trace their descent from Abraham (the first through his son Isaac, the second through Ishmael). God's promise was also conditional upon the Jews obeying certain laws. The Jews were first exiled from Palestine because they disobeyed God, so some Jews even regard modern Israel as wrong because the conditions for God's promise being fulfilled have not yet been met.

The Dome of the Rock, on the left of this picture, is one of the world's most beautiful Islamic mosques. Beneath it stands the impressive Western Wall, an important Jewish place of prayer.

Those Jews and Christians who try to justify today's wars and political struggles in religious terms, however, represent a tiny minority whose support for often violent extremism has attracted few sympathizers. On the Arab, Muslim side – not forgetting that about ten percent of Palestine's Arab population is Christian – the struggle for Palestine has in the past been conducted mainly on a political level. After the revolution in Iran in 1979, there was a rise in Islamic fundamentalism and in Arab religious militancy, but here again it has been confined to a minority whose hostility is directed against the Western world generally.

A series of occupations

Historically, the Jewish claim to Palestine rests on Jewish habitation from about 1300 B.C., when the tribes of Israel, escaping under Moses' leadership from Egypt, entered and conquered Palestine from the Canaanites, Philistines (from whose the name Palestine is derived), and other tribes who were living there. Jewish rule continued until the sixth century B.C., when the regional empires of Assyria and Babylon destroyed the Jewish kingdoms and exiled many Jews. The Romans captured Palestine in 63 B.C., and, following a Jew-

This stone relief records the destruction of the Jewish Temple in Jerusalem during the Roman occupation.

Turkish Ottoman troops in Palestine in 1917. From A.D. 1517, the Turkish ruled Palestine for 400 years.

ish revolt against Rome in A.D. 132, the Emperor Hadrian forbade Jews to enter Jerusalem on pain of death. This was the end of Jewish national independence in Palestine until the State of Israel was founded in 1948, although Jews have always lived there in small numbers.

The Palestinians are a mixture of the many peoples and empires that have invaded and ruled the land since Roman

In March 1918, British troops marched through Es Salt as part of the British occupation of Palestine at the end of World War I.

times. The Arab conquests of the seventh century A.D. rendered Palestine, in common with surrounding countries, Arab in culture and language, although parts of Palestine were ruled by the European Crusaders in the twelfth and the thirteenth centuries. Palestine was part of the Turkish Ottoman Empire from 1517 until it was occupied by British forces in 1918.

4
The birth of Zionism

Zionism, the political movement aimed at founding a Jewish state in Palestine, began as a reaction to the anti-Semitism in Europe, which in the nineteenth century erupted into increasingly violent persecution of Jews, particularly in Russia and eastern Europe. Zionism's founder, Theodor Herzl (1860–1904), was a Hungarian Jew who believed anti-Semitism would occur in any nation that contained Jews among its people. In 1896, he wrote: "Let the sovereignty be

Theodor Herzl, the founder of Zionism.

granted us over a portion of the globe large enough to satisfy the rightful requirements of a nation; the rest we shall manage for ourselves."

Herzl had no preference for Palestine as the site of a Jewish state – other sites considered were in Africa and South America – but he realized that the emotional attraction of Palestine could be a powerful force if harnessed to his political ideology. Herzl's ideas were received enthusiastically, and led to the first Zionist Congress in Basle in 1897, which adopted a program for "the establishment of a publicly and legally secured home in Palestine for the Jewish people."

Zionist immigrants

The first large wave of Jewish emigration to Palestine – called *Aliyah* ("ascent") in Hebrew – started in 1882, part of the great exodus of Jews fleeing repression in eastern Europe. They lived mainly off charitable subsidies from abroad. At that time, there were already about 24,000 Jews, themselves mostly immigrants, in Palestine, compared with an Arab population of over 500,000.

The second wave, around the turn of the century, arrived armed with Herzl's doctrines, determined to establish themselves as an economically independent community. Their first task was to bring the land under Jewish ownership, so in 1901 a worldwide organization, the Jewish National Fund (JNF), was set up. The Zionist immigrants brought with them socialist ideas from eastern Europe, and they set about establishing collective, egalitarian settlements, called *kibbutzim*, to farm the land. Although only a small number joined these settlements, most immigrants were sympathetic to the aims of the socialist Zionists, who advocated Jewish self-reliance through productive, manual labor and envisaged a welfare state in which trade unionism would play a major role. These ideas, which came to be known as Labor Zionism, dominated Israeli political life until 1977.

The casualties of Zionism

Another aspect of Zionism, however, was its almost total lack of provision or concern for the native Arab population of Palestine. After visiting Palestine in 1891, one Russian Jew wrote: "We abroad have got used to thinking that Eretz Israel (the land of Israel) is today totally desolate, an uncul-

tivated wilderness, and that anyone who wishes to buy land there can do so to his heart's content. But this is not in fact the case. It is difficult to find any uncultivated land anywhere in this country. . . ."

It was, and remains, a JNF principle that land acquired by Jews in Palestine must never be sold or leased to non-Jews. The Zionist ideal of the "conquest of labor" stipulated that only Jews should work the land that Jews acquired. Even Herzl realized reluctantly that this was impossible to achieve without depriving the native inhabitants, at least seventy-five percent of whom were peasants, of their land and livelihoods.

Galilee, 1904, one of the first groups of Jewish watchmen. Armed guards were as necessary to the settlers and farmers.

The initial Zionist safeguard against a threat from the native population was to incorporate the heroic image of the Jewish soldier alongside that of the Jewish farmer. Many Jewish immigrants, however, left Palestine when they realized that their settlement could be continued only by force at the expense of the native population.

5
The "Arab Awakening"

The other principal force in the Palestine conflict is Arab nationalism, yet it is hard to trace its evolution. The concept of dividing the Middle East into nation states under non-religious governments was a wholly alien idea introduced into the Arab world by the European colonial powers. At the time when the first Jewish settlers were arriving in Palestine, the idea that the Middle East could or should be so

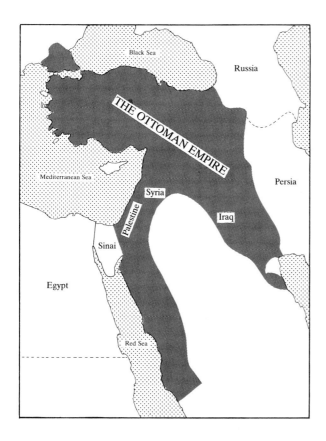

For four centuries, the Ottoman Empire dominated the Middle East and Palestinian Arabs looked to the Ottoman Sultan as the source of all earthly authority.

divided was undreamed of by its Arab inhabitants. The Arabs thought of themselves first and foremost as Muslims, as citizens of the wider Islamic community (*Umma* in Arabic). The ultimate, if often nominal, source of all authority other than God's rested where it had for the last four centuries – with the Ottoman Sultan in Constantinople (modern-day Istanbul).

The growth of Arab nationalism

This is not to say there was no impetus for change. Ever since Napolean invaded and occupied Egypt from 1798–1801, the Arabs have been trying to cope with the new era being physically thrust upon them by the Western powers, busy competing with one another to expand their empires. The French invaded Algeria in 1830; the British occupied Aden in 1839 and Egypt in 1882; the French, Tunisia in 1881; the Italians seized Libya in 1911. The Arabs responded to these threats by trying to unite against them in a pan-Islamic movement, as expounded by Jamal al-Din al-Afghani (1839–97), who laid the seeds for Arab nationalism. Those inspired by al-Afghani began to blame the backwardness and weakness of the Islamic world, in relation to the West, on their history of mismanagement by the Ottoman Turks.

Those involved with this "Arab Awakening" still looked to the Ottoman Empire for protection from the West, but wanted to reform and strengthen their community and escape Turkish cultural domination by returning the Arabs

Kaiser Wilhelm II of Germany on his arrival in Constantinople in 1917. Fearful of Germany's alliance with Turkey, the British invaded Palestine in World War I.

Sharif Husein Ibn Ali (1856–1931), ruler of the Islamic holy city of Mecca, founded a new Arabian dynasty.

to the leadership of Islam. By the turn of the century, the Ottoman Empire was challenged by both the forces of European expansionism from without and by non-Muslim minorities from within.

Revolt against Turkish rule

The outbreak of World War I in 1914, in which Turkey sided with Germany, forced Britain to protect its interests in the region, above all the Suez Canal in Egypt. Sharif Husein ibn Ali, ruler of the Islamic holy city of Mecca in the Arabian peninsula, seemed ideal as the Arabs' leader and an ally against the Turks. Negotiations between the British High Commissioner in Egypt, Sir Henry McMahon, and the Sharif, in which the Arabs were led to believe that, in return for their support in the war, they would be given control of what is today Israel, Syria, Lebanon, Iraq, and Saudi Arabia, led Husein to side with Britain in June 1916 and organize an Arab revolt against Turkish rule.

6
The Balfour Declaration

Britain encouraged the Arab independence movement but had no intention of giving the Arabs the power they had been promised once the Turks, with invaluable Arab help, had been defeated. In May 1916, a secret Anglo-French-Russian accord, known as the Sykes–Picot Agreement, divided between France and Britain all the areas promised to the Arabs, apart from the sparsely populated desert regions.

The Sykes-Picot Agreement was named after its English and French negotiators who secretly agreed to divide any land captured from the Turks between themselves. The Allied Condominium (area of joint rule) almost coincides with the area of Israel today.

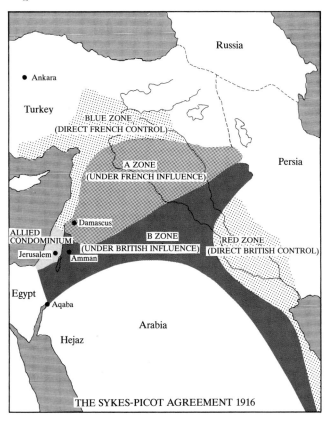

THE SYKES-PICOT AGREEMENT 1916

The Arabs' sense of betrayal when they discovered that they had only exchanged one set of foreign rulers for another was never forgotten. Nowhere was this sense of betrayal more bitter than in the case of Palestine, which the British Army under General Allenby captured from the Turks in 1917–18. At the end of World War I, after thirty-two years of concentrated effort 56,000 Jews, according to the British census of 1918, had been settled in Palestine on some two percent of its land area. British rule was the opportunity for the Zionist movement to turn what was still only a dream into reality. The lobbying of Chaim Weizmann, a Russian

1917. The Mayor of Jerusalem surrenders the city to a British soldier as World War I draws to a close.

Jew who later became Israel's first president, persuaded the British government to issue a document in 1917 that changed the course of Middle East history. In the form of a letter from the British foreign secretary, Lord Balfour, to a prominent English Jew, Lord Rothschild, it stated that: "His Majesty's Government view with favour the establishment in Palestine of a national home for the Jewish people." However it went on to add that "nothing shall be done which may prejudice the civil and religious rights of existing non-Jewish communities in Palestine."

The unworkable mandate

In 1920, at the League of Nations Supreme Council meeting in San Remo, Britain was assigned the mandate for Palestine, which carried with it the obligation to implement the

Palestine, May, 1918. Dr. Chaim Weizmann arriving at the British government's headquarters in Palestine.

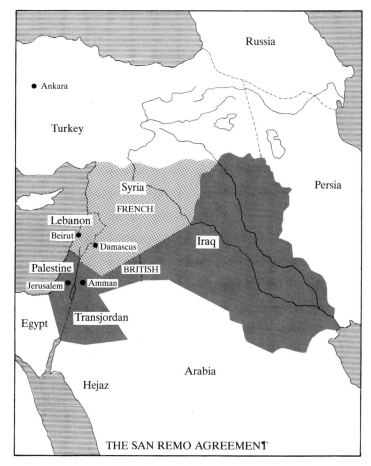

The division of land, following the San Remo agreement in 1920, gave Britain the mandate for guiding Palestine toward independence.

THE SAN REMO AGREEMENT

Balfour Declaration. The League of Nations mandate system was devised as a means for nondeveloped countries to be guided to independence and self-government with the help of the industrialized nations. But Lord Balfour's views on Palestine were contained in a secret memorandum to the British Cabinet in 1919 which said that: "... in Palestine we do not propose even to go through the form of consulting the wishes of the present inhabitants of the country ... Zionism, be it right or wrong, good or bad, is ... of far profounder import than the desires and prejudices of the 700,000 Arabs who now inhabit that ancient land ... In short, so far as Palestine is concerned, the Powers have made no ... declaration of policy which they have not always intended to violate."

7
The Zionists betrayed

Jaffa was the scene of much rioting both in the 1920s and, as shown here, in the 1930s. Native Palestinians and Jewish settlers fought for supremacy while the British Army tried to keep the peace.

Palestine under the British mandate was the scene of increasingly violent confrontations between the Jewish settlers and the Palestinians. In 1921, riots in Jaffa left 200 Jews and 120 Arabs dead or wounded. Although they outnumbered the Jews, the Palestinians had no political organization or experience with which to assert their own presence in the country. The Zionists had not only the support and sympathy of the British authorities but also an efficient political machine. In addition they soon began training the *Hagannah* – forerunner of the Israeli Army.

By 1929, there were 156,000 immigrants owning four percent of the total area of Palestine, but fourteen percent of its cultivable land. Palestinian fears that the Jews were planning to seize total power erupted into widespread violence in 1929; in one incident over sixty Jewish members of a religious community in Hebron were massacred by Arabs. A British commission of inquiry found that the causes of Arab unrest were Jewish immigration and land settlement which should therefore be curtailed. However, this was overruled by the British prime minister, Ramsay MacDonald.

The situation worsened in the economic depression of the 1930s. Landless and workless Palestinians began to drift

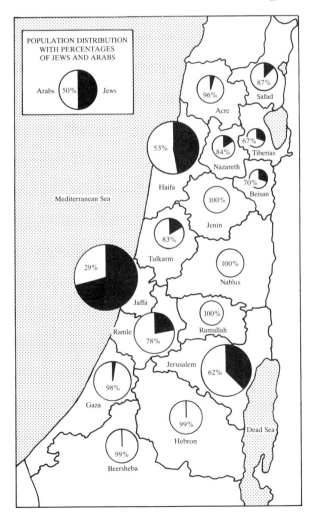

Palestine, 1946. This map, prepared by a British committee attempting to solve Palestine's problems, shows a concentration of Jews in wealthier areas.

to the outskirts of the urban, industralized centers being developed by the Jewish immigrants; some were given menial, low-paid jobs. In April 1936, the Palestinians formed an Arab Higher Committee, which called for a general strike in protest at Jewish immigration. This turned into a spontaneous popular unprising against Britain and the Zionists.

The cost of Arab rebellion

In 1937, another British inquiry found that the mandate was unworkable and recommended precisely what the Palestinians were fighting to avert – the partition of their country into a Jewish and an Arab state. It was an admission that Britain could not easily establish a Jewish homeland in Palestine *and* protect the rights of Palestinians.

Jewish immigrants feeling Nazi persecution in Europe were by then arriving in unprecedented numbers – the United States and western Europe having refused to admit the bulk of the refugees. In 1938, Arab guerrillas seized effective control in some areas. The *Hagannah*, now much expanded and better equipped with smuggled arms, began not just to defend Jewish settlements from Arab attack but

Jerusalem, 1985. Since the unemployment of the 1930s, Palestinians have been forced by poverty to seek menial work from Israeli employers on an irregular basis.

to launch counterattacks. A small extremist faction split from the *Hagannah* to form the *Irgun Zvai Leumi* (National Military Organization), and mount terrorist operations despite condemnation by Zionist leaders.

The Arab rebellion was finally crushed in early 1939 by the British Army. It had cost the lives of 101 British soldiers, 463 Jews, and an estimated 5,000 Palestinians. But with war looming in Europe, Britain was desperately trying to avoid committing much-needed forces to suppress the Palestinians.

Israel maintains a People's Army by conscripting all young people. After training they are always liable to be recalled. Women must be prepared to fight alongside men, as in this target practice.

Palestine – A binational state?
In May 1939, the British government issued a White Paper envisaging the creation of a binational state in Palestine in ten years and limitation of Jewish immigration to 75,000 over the next five years, after which no further immigrants would be admitted without Palestinian approval. The Palestinians at that time formed about two-thirds of the population. The White Paper was furiously denounced as a betrayal by the Zionists.

8
The end of the mandate

Jerusalem, 1946. Rubble and desolation were all that remained after the King David Hotel had been torn apart by Zionist explosives.

The Arab revolt of 1936–39 also saw the rise of the militarist aspect of Zionism. Vladimir Jabotinsky, founder of the *Hagannah*, had suggested that "the only way to liberate the country is by the sword," and in this groups like the *Irgun* took the lead. During World War II, there was a truce between Zionist and British forces, but with Britain preventing further Jewish immigration to Palestine, Hitler's defeat ushered in a change of policy. On July 22, 1946, the *Irgun*,

under the leadership of Menachem Begin, later prime minister of Israel, smuggled explosives into the headquarters of Britain's administration in Palestine, the King David Hotel in Jerusalem. Eighty-eight people (Britons, Jews and Arabs) were killed in the explosion. It was a message to the world that the Jews of Palestine were now ready to seize statehood by force if necessary.

In the wake of the Holocaust

World War II had, of course, completely changed the way this message was received. The systematic murder of six million Jews in the Nazi Holocaust secured near universal support for the Zionist effort to give the Jews of the world a new, safe future in an independent state in Palestine. For Britain, caught in a web of violence by its conflicting promises to the Zionists and the Arabs, it was not so simple. The foreign secretary of the new Labour government, Ernest Bevin, attempted to remain impartial. Sticking to the 1939 White Paper, he rejected a Zionist demand for the immediate admission to Palestine of 100,000 Jewish survivors of the Holocaust. But postwar Britain was no longer a major power abroad. Nor could the war-weary British public afford a long Zionist campaign of violence. Knowing this, the Zionists sought political support from the new world power, the United States, and prepared for all-out war with the Arabs once Britain decided to pull out.

An end to British authority

Anti-British feeling was evoked worldwide by newsreels showing British troops turning away the pathetic victims of Hitler's concentration camps from "the Promised Land." In the United States, the large and influential Jewish community mobilized itself to persuade the government to back the Zionists wholeheartedly. Britain was heavily indebted to, and dependent on, the United States as a result of the war, and pressure from Washington on top of the anti-British terrorism of the *Irgun* and its offshoot, *Stern*, was too much. In April 1947, the British government turned to the United Nations for help. On November 29, the United Nations General Assembly, after strong American pressure on many smaller nations, voted 33–13, with ten abstentions, to partition Palestine into Arab and Jewish states, with Jerusalem remaining under international control.

   This partition plan, which allocated fifty-seven percent

In November 1947, the United Nations drew up a partition plan for the division of Palestine into Jewish and Arab homelands, but neither group approved the division.

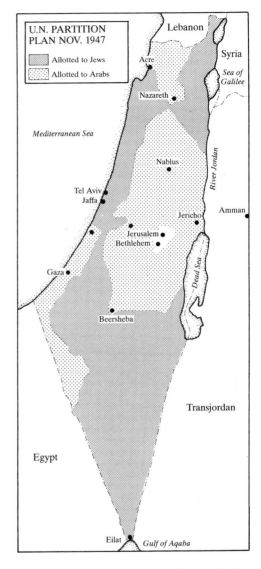

U.N. PARTITION PLAN NOV. 1947

▨ Allotted to Jews
░ Allotted to Arabs

Lebanon

Syria

Acre

Sea of Galilee

Nazareth

Mediterranean Sea

Nablus

River Jordan

Tel Aviv
Jaffa

Jericho

Amman

Jerusalem
Bethlehem

Dead Sea

Gaza

Beersheba

Transjordan

Egypt

Eilat   Gulf of Aqaba

of the territory, including the most fertile, to the Jews (thirty-three percent of the population), was immediately rejected by the Arabs, who protested that the General Assembly was not competent to partition a country against the wishes of the majority of its inhabitants. Britain refused to enforce the decision, and announced it would relinquish its mandate for Palestine on May 15, 1948.

Even under the partition plan, the population ratio meant that the proposed Jewish state would have a slight Arab majority. This was at odds with the principles of Zionism. The head of Jewish colonization in Palestine, Joseph Weitz, wrote in 1940: "Between ourselves it must be clear that there is no room for both peoples together in this country ... We shall not achieve our goal of being an independent people with the Arabs in this small country. The only solution is a Palestine, at least Western Palestine (west of the Jordan River) without Arabs ... And there is no other way than to transfer the Arabs from here to the neighboring countries, to transfer all of them; not one village, not one tribe should be left."

A shipload of immigrants arriving in Haifa in 1949.

Revisionist Zionists, like the *Irgun* and *Stern*, were willing to use terrorism to get rid of the unwanted Palestinians. On April 9, 1948, Begin's *Irgun* troops descended on the hitherto peaceful Arab village of Deir Yassin and massacred 254 of its civilian inhabitants. Begin himself described the "unexpected and momentous consequences" thus: "Arabs throughout the country, induced to believe wild tales of '*Irgun* butchery,' were seized with panic and started to flee

After the Zionists had seized the land vacated by fleeing Palestinians in 1948, they occupied a greater area of land than the UN Partition plan had proposed. (See map on page 40.)

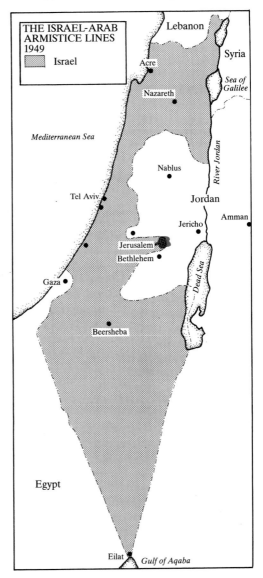

THE ISRAEL-ARAB ARMISTICE LINES 1949

Israel

Lebanon

Syria

Acre

Sea of Galilee

Nazareth

Mediterranean Sea

Nablus

River Jordan

Tel Aviv

Jordan

Jericho

Amman

Jerusalem

Bethlehem

Dead Sea

Gaza

Beersheba

Egypt

Eilat

Gulf of Aqaba

for their lives ... Of the about 800,000 Arabs who lived on the present territory of the State of Israel, only some 165,000 are still there.''

The assault on Deir Yassin was part of a military plan by Zionist forces to capture as much territory as possible before the British withdrew. Their well-armed and well-trained troops met little resistance from the ill-prepared Palestinians, 300,00 of whom fled. Large areas designated for the proposed Arab state, as well as parts of Jerusalem, were seized. British forces did not intervene and the last soldier left as planned when the mandate expired on May 14. As it did, Chaim Weizmann raised the emblem of the Star of David and proclaimed the new State of Israel.

Jerusalem, February 1949. At age 74, Chaim Weizmann was sworn in as Israel's first president.

9
The Suez Crisis

Palestine, May 1948. As soon as the British Mandate expired, Egyptian and Transjordan troops invaded Palestine to stem a Zionist occupation. Here, soldiers of the Arab Legion take up a defense position.

Had not bordering Arab states intervened militarily in support of the Palestinians when the State of Israel was proclaimed, there is little doubt that the Zionist forces would have gone on to occupy the whole country. As it was, Arab forces were still heavily defeated by the *Hagannah*. East Jerusalem, the West Bank, defended by the British-trained Arab Legion, and the semidesert Gaza Strip to the south, which had been held by the Egyptian Army – about twenty percent of the land in all – was all that was left of Palestine in Arab hands.

An estimated 800,000 – over half the entire Arab population of Palestine – were expelled and made homeless, and
none has since been allowed by Israel to return, despite
repeated UN resolutions. Makeshift camps on Israel's
borders were set up for them by a UN organization, the
United Nations Relief and Works Agency (UNRWA), spe-
cially formed to try to cope with the desperate problems
caused by so many destitute people. Over 600,000 Palestinians still live in UNRWA camps today. Only some 165,000
Palestinians were left in the area now occupied by the Israeli
state. Many Zionists leaders abhorred the terror tactics
employed by the extremists among them to induce so many
to flee, but could not bring themselves to reverse the coup
thus achieved.

*Palestinian refugees
of the 1948 war were
forced, like this
couple, to seek
shelter in tents or
caves.*

Tel Aviv, January 1949. Jewish police and army personnel search Arabs before allowing them to enter an Arab village.

In 1950, the Arab League states decided to continue a blockade which had been imposed during World War II, indefinitely. The anger of the Arabs at the treatment of the Palestinians, and their defeat, which mocked their newly won independence from Europe, brought radical leaders to power in many of the Arab states, who considered the task of Arab national liberation incomplete while Palestine remained under Israeli rule.

In the meantime, Israel destroyed Arab villages and changed their names. The Israeli justification for this "Judaization" was summed up when in 1969 Israel's prime minister, Golda Meir, declared: "It was not as though there was a Palestinian people in Palestine ... and we came and ... took their country away from them. They did not exist."

The rise of Egypt under Nasser

Meanwhile immigration increased as the large Jewish communities of the Arab world had their centuries-old status as a tolerated minority jeopardized by the conflict with Israel. Some 500,000 Oriental Jews left the Arab countries for Israel during the 1950s. Today they form the majority of Israel's Jewish population.

Just as the Israelis in the 1950s and 1960s tried to erase all signs of Palestinian identity, so in Lebanon in 1982 a Palestinian tries to remove the Star of David from a street in West Beirut.

47

The majority of Israel's Jewish inhabitants today are Oriental Jews – like this couple – who emigrated from surrounding Arab countries.

In 1954, a radical Arab nationalist, Gamal Abd an-Nasser, came to power after a coup in Israel's potentially most powerful Arab neighbor, Egypt. Nasser was seen to be a threat not just to the West, as a potential instrument of the USSR, but to Britain in particular, who still directly controlled the strategic and profitable Suez Canal. Denied Western arms to counter Israel's growing strength, and refused development funds which had been promised by Britain and the United States, Nasser won support from Arabs everywhere by defiantly announcing the nationalization of the Canal in July 1956.

The thwarted invasion of Suez
Incidents along the Egyptian–Israeli border led Israel to share Europe's hostility to Egypt and a secret Anglo–French–Israeli agreement was concluded. Israel invaded Egypt's Sinai peninsula on October 29 and quickly reached the east bank of the Canal. A joint Anglo-French force then invaded

Egypt to occupy the Canal zone, ostensibly to secure the waterway for international shipping but in reality to topple Nasser. However, this plan failed. Nasser was not overthrown but celebrated as an Arab hero; the French and British were quickly forced to withdraw under American pressure, leaving the Canal completely in Egyptian hands; and anti-Western feelings intensified throughout the Middle East. Israel, whose role as an instrument of Western imperialism was strengthened in Arab minds by the affair, did manage to end the Egyptian blockade on Israeli shipping in the Straits of Tiran, but it was later forced to withdraw from Sinai by American President Eisenhower's threat of economic sanctions.

Alexandria, July 1956. After announcing that he had nationalized the Suez Canal, Nasser became the people's hero.

10
The 1967 War

Egypt, June 1967. Having shot down an Egyptian fighter, Israeli soldiers inspect the wreckage.

To provide a safe outlet for Palestinian frustration, the Arab states in 1964 created the Palestine Liberation Organization (PLO) as an official body of the Arab League. One group of Palestinians, with little faith in the Arab governments, founded their own organization, known as *Fatah* ("Victory"). Under the leadership of Yasser Arafat, the *fedayeen* ("self-sacrificers") of *Fatah* began military operations in 1965, which increased Arab–Israeli tension. With the exception of Syria, all the Arab states bordering Israel did their best to suppress the activities of *Fatah*, which they feared could drag them unprepared into a war with Israel.

But the Arab governments, trapped by their own boastful

anti-Israel rhetoric, could not be seen to continue evading the situation. Syria led the way toward confrontation, a path that Nasser's Egypt, the powerhouse of Arab nationalism, could hardly do other than follow. Syria countered Israel's scheme to divert the waters of the Jordan for irrigation purposes and bombed Israeli settlements trying to expand cultivation in the Golan Heights border area. In May 1967, Nasser received a warning of an imminent Israeli attack on Syria, so he sent Egyptian forces into Sinai and reimposed the blockade on the Straits of Tiran. On June 5, Israel destroyed most of Egypt's air force on the ground in a surprise attack, and reoccupied Sinai. In just six days, Jordan, who had entered the war on Egypt's side, was also defeated, and the Old City of Jerusalem and the West Bank occupied by Israeli forces. In the north, the Golan Heights were captured from Syria. In addition to Egyptian Sinai and Syrian Golan, all of Palestine was now in Israel's hands. Another 250,000 Palestinians fled their country, mostly across the Jordan River.

Arabs from the West Bank of the Jordan River fled across the demolished Allenby Bridge into East Jordan during the 1967 hostilities. By mid-1968, some 450,000 persons had crossed this borderline, most of them ending up in UNRWA refugee camps.

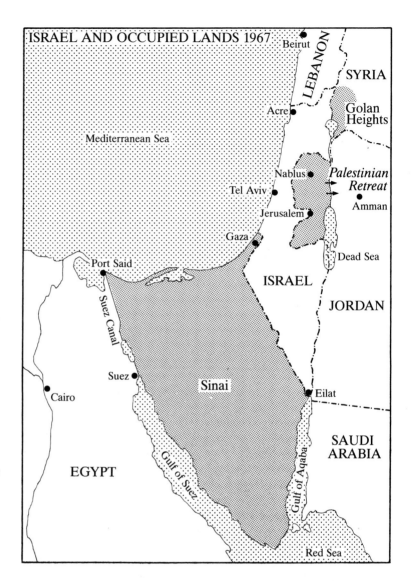

ISRAEL AND OCCUPIED LANDS 1967

The additional area Israel occupied in 1967 was declared to be illegal by United Nations Resolution 242, because it was acquired by warfare rather than by negotiation.

Israel's parliament, the Knesset, passed a law incorporating the predominantly Arab Old City of Jerusalem, into one city under Israeli rule, an annexation unanimously declared to be illegal by the UN General Assembly on July 4, 1967. The rest of the newly conquered territory kept the status of occupied areas. UN Resolution 242 (see page 73), adopted unanimously by the Security Council on November 22, 1967, stressed that territory was not to be acquired by war. Israel, Egypt, Jordan, and Lebanon accepted Resolu-

52

tion 242, but Syria and Iraq rejected it because its terms implied recognition and acceptance of Israel.

Israel's subsequent actions contradicted its claim that its conquests were not expansionist. As with the territory it had captured in 1948, it again seized land, exiled inhabitants, destroyed Arab villages, and began to establish Jewish settlements. But unlike the 1948 war, despite the second Palestinian exodus, the territories acquired in 1967 still contained a large Arab population: East Jerusalem, the West

In 1967, Israeli soldiers began conducting a rigid house-to-house census to establish who now inhabited the Gaza Strip.

Three fedayeen Palestinian guerrillas who fought King Hussein's forces during the Jordanian civil war. They are pictured here in front of a bullet-torn Palestinian flag.

Bank, and the Gaza Strip between them contained close to one million Palestinians. Outright annexation would have jeopardized Israel's Jewish majority by adding so many more Arab citizens to the state, so even limited rights of citizenship, similar to those granted to Arabs within Israel's 1948 borders, were withheld.

Arafat's PLO in Jordan

The shattering defeat of 1967 caused disillusioned Palestinian refugees to abandon hope of assistance from the Arab states and join the guerrillas of the *Fatah* movement, which consequently stepped up its military operations. In March 1968, 300 *Fatah* guerrillas successfully repulsed an Israeli reprisal raid of 15,000 troops, supported by tanks, aimed at the Karameh refugee camp in Jordan. Within a year, *Fatah* had taken over control of the PLO, and Arafat was elected chairman – a post he has held ever since. Other Palestinian groups sprang up, such as the Marxist–Leninist Popular Front for the Liberation of Palestine (PFLP), and the Democratic Front for the Liberation of Palestine

(DFLP), both led by Palestinian Christians and committed to spreading revolution throughout the Middle East as the first step to liberating Palestine.

But in Jordan, where most Palestinian refugees had ended up, and which inevitably became the PLO's headquarters, it was the government of King Hussein that was threatened by the growing strength of the guerrillas, and the heavy Israeli reprisals they attracted. The hijacking of airliners to Jordan by the PFLP in September 1970 finally induced Hussein to act before the Palestinians, who outnumbered native Jordanians, took over his country completely. After a bloody war in which at least 2,000 Palestinians were killed, Hussein's troops crushed the *fedayeen* movement in Jordan.

Black September
This ushered in the phase of terrorism that first focused the world's attention on the Palestinians. A group calling itself Black September assassinated the Jordanian prime minister in November 1971, and achieved worldwide notoriety with the killing of eleven Israeli athletes at the Munich Olympics in September 1972. In reprisal, the Israeli Air Force killed an estimated 400 Palestinians in camps in Lebanon, which was emerging as the next major base for Palestinian guerrillas after their expulsion from Jordan.

Israel used sophisticated technology to seal its borders, within which the only Palestinian community to achieve any measure of armed resistance, that of the crowded refugee camps of Gaza, was brutally suppressed in the early 1970s.

An exiled community in Lebanon
Although the PLO had no notable military success after the Battle of Karameh, it continued to command the support of Palestinians everywhere, embodying both their ideal of national independence and their hope of returning to Palestine. In Lebanon, reluctant host to some 300,000 Palestinian refugees, the PLO organized social, medical, and educational services, giving the exiles the dignity of self-reliance. Above all, the Palestinian people acknowledged no one else as qualified to represent them in any negotiaion over their future. In the past, Israel had dismissed the PLO as "terrorist gangs" and seen its goal of a secular, democratic state in Palestine for Jews and Arabs alike as no more than a propaganda device to cloak its true aim to kill all Jewish citizens in Israel.

11
The Camp David Treaty

On October 6, 1973, when Israel was celebrating the Jewish holy day of Yom Kippur, war broke out again. A simultaneous attack by Egyptian forces across the Suez Canal and an armored thrust across the Golan Heights by Syria took the Israelis completely by surprise. The Egyptians outflanked Israel's "impregnable" fortifications on the west

Israel struck back at Syria, in the area shown here, after the Syrian and Egyptian invasions of the 1973 war. The buffer zones on Israel's borders were revealed to be less impregnanable than had once been believed.

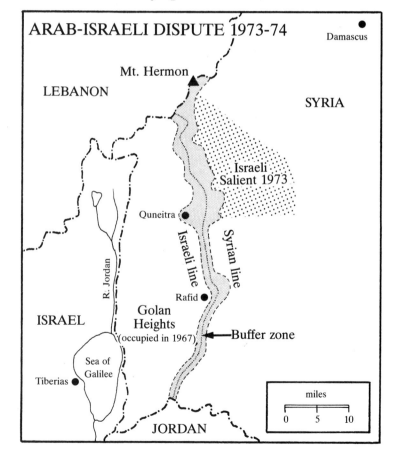

ARAB-ISRAELI DISPUTE 1973-74

Damascus

Mt. Hermon

LEBANON

SYRIA

Israeli Salient 1973

Quneitra

Israeli line

Syrian line

R. Jordan

Rafid

ISRAEL

Golan Heights
(occupied in 1967)

Buffer zone

Sea of Galilee

Tiberias

miles

0   5   10

JORDAN

bank of the Canal within hours, as Syrian tanks plunged deep into Israeli-held territory. As the Israelis desperately mobilized their people's army for a counterattack, it became clear that the conflict now carried dangerous consequences for the whole world. Superpower involvement was such that the risk of a direct confrontation between the US and the USSR loomed ominously close. Russian arms supplied the Arab camp, as the latest American technology poured into Israel. Bolstered by the latter, Israel's military supremacy reasserted itself and its army struck back at Egypt and Syria, threatening their capitals. Direct American–Soviet negotiations forced a ceasefire on October 23, and the immediate crisis receded, but not before Washington had placed its nuclear forces worldwide on Defense Condition Three to deter Soviet intervention.

Arab losses were severe, with over 20,000 killed. Israel, with 2,800 dead, lost a greater proportion of a smaller population, but the biggest shock of all was the end of the myth

After the Yom Kippur War, Israel treated Egypt with more respect. In 1977, President Sadat visited Jerusalem for peace talks and is seen here with Israeli ex-Prime Minister Golda Meir.

of Israeli invincibility. The October, or Yom Kippur War, devised by Nasser's successor, President Sadat, earned Egypt the right to negotiate with a chastened Israel as an equal. It also gave the West a direct incentive to find a solution, not just because of the frightening danger to world peace, but because the Arab oil-producing states together imposed a devastatingly effective oil blockade on industrialized nations supporting Israel.

A gun or an olive branch?

One result of this was a new respect for the Arabs, especially from European nations dependent on imported energy. There was now a new willingness to listen to the Arab side of the conflict. The Arab governments, however, had long since realized that Israel was dependent on American economic and political aid so it was to Washington, not Moscow, that Sadat now looked for the means of reclaiming Egypt's Sinai peninsula.

On September 21, 1974, the UN General Assembly raised the Palestine question for the first time since the creation of Israel. Yasser Arafat was invited to address the debate and told the delegates he came bearing a gun and an olive branch. It was for the Israelis to decide which he was to use. The following month an Arab summit meeting confirmed the PLO as "sole legitimate representative of the Palestinian people," and King Hussein formally relinquished to the PLO his claim on the Israeli-occupied West Bank. The PLO agreed to establish a "national authority" on any Palestinian territory from which Israel withdrew, but this willingness to lower its sights from a secular democratic state in all of Palestine to a "mini-state," coexisting alongside Israel in the territories occupied in 1967 was a highly divisive move within the PLO. The result was a split between the moderates – Arafat and the mainstream *Fatah* – and the smaller, hardline factions, who came to be associated with the "rejectionist front" Arab states, like Libya and Syria.

The PLO "state" in Lebanon

In 1975, civil war broke out in Lebanon. There had always been hostility between Lebanon's many Christian and Muslim sects, but from the start of the Arab–Israeli conflict the Palestinians were a key factor in the civil violence. As in Jordan before 1970, the presence of armed Palestinians in Lebanon drew Israeli attacks. Being mostly Muslim, the

جماجم لبنان!!"" تراس "الإخوان"

This 1982 cartoon, from a right-wing Christian Phalangist newspaper in Beirut, shows the price of creating a mini Palestinian state in West Beirut. Yasser Arafat's sign of victory is undercut by the Labanese skulls surrounding him.

Palestinians also upset the country's volatile political mix. The lack of any central authority in Lebanon allowed the PLO to establish what amounted to a "state within a state," with its headquarters in West Beirut and military bases in the south, close to Israel's border. For this the Palestinians paid the heavy price of a bitter war with Lebanon's Christian militia – trained, armed, and financed by Israel to counteract the influence of the PLO. The destruction of the PLO "state" in Lebanon was the aim of the 1982 Israeli invasion.

Egyptian President Anwar Sadat, American President Jimmy Carter, and Israeli Prime Minister Menachem Begin, preparing to sign a peace treaty at Camp David in March 1979.

On November 19, 1977, President Sadat of Egypt flew to Jerusalem to negotiate peace directly with Israel. On March 26, 1979, at Camp David in the United States, an Israeli–Egyptian peace treaty was signed, formally ending the state of war between the two countries. Its main provisions were the withdrawal of Israeli forces from Sinai over a three-year period and the negotiation of a "self-governing authority" for the Palestinians of the West Bank and Gaza. The Camp David Treaty seemed to be the crowning success of American President Carter's term in office. For the other Arab states, it was a betrayal – the separate peace they had all vowed never to make. Egypt was boycotted and expelled from the Arab League, whose members felt that she had sacrificed the Palestinian cause and Arab unity for American aid and weapons and to regain Sinai. The Palestinians themselves led the crusade against Camp David and "the traitor Sadat," denouncing the proposed scheme for Palestinian autonomy as a device to legitimize and make permanent Israel's occupation of the West Bank and Gaza Strip. Particularly galling to the Arabs was the fact that Egypt had negotiated with an Israeli government headed by Menachem Begin, who had defeated the Labor Party for the first time in Israel's history in May 1977. Begin, notorious for his terrorist involvement in expelling the Arab population of Palestine, admitted that his right-wing, revisionist brand of Zionism included the expansion of Israeli territory.

Begin's territorial expansion

When Begin came to power there were 5,000 Israeli settlers in 36 outposts in the occupied territories; when he resigned there were 27,500 in 114 settlements, and approximately half the land had been confiscated from its Arab owners. The aim of the settlement policy, condemned universally as both illegal under international law and as a recipe for permanent Israeli–Palestinian conflict, was to preempt the establishment of a Palestinian state there. Begin's government was also criticized for its attack on Iraq's nuclear plant in June 1981, and for annexing the Syrian Golan Heights in December of the same year.

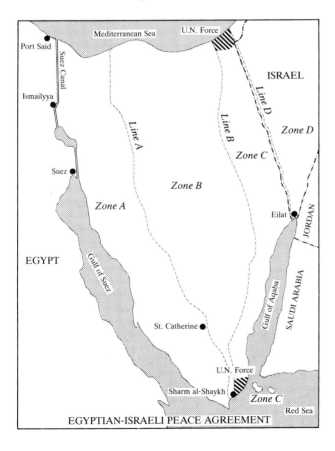

EGYPTIAN-ISRAELI PEACE AGREEMENT

The terms of the Camp David Peace Treaty demanded a withdrawal of Israeli forces from Egypt in three annual phases, as these three zones indicate.

12
Israel today

Israel today is both the fulfillment of Zionism and its failure. A sovereign Jewish state has been created in Palestine, and under Israel's "Law of Return" any Jew in the world may settle there and be granted automatic citizenship. While early Zionists saw the Jews of the world flocking to join the new state, the large majority have always opted to stay in the Diaspora (to settle outside Israel). Today Israel's Jewish population of 3.5 million is declining. Far from being the ultimate refuge, Israel, with its incessant wars, is probably the most dangerous place on earth for a Jew to live. The unremitting hostility of its neighbors has denied Israel

Not all young Israelis support the Zionist program of expansion into Arab territories. This demonstration in Tel Aviv in 1982 was mounted by both Palestinians and Jews.

the opportunity to participate in regional trade and commerce, as well as forcing her to spend over twenty-five percent of her total budget on defense. The Zionist goal of Jewish self-reliance has never been attained. Since its inception, Israel has survived on subsidies from the Diaspora. The United States now provides more economic and military aid for Israel than for any other country. Israeli society today is deeply divided over the country's future. Many opposed the Lebanon war both because of the large-scale killing of civilians and because they regarded it as the first war fought for reasons other than self-defense. The 1967 conquests made Israel military ruler over more than a million Arabs, transforming the Jews from the oppressed to the oppressors.

Israel is far from a safe homeland for its Jewish inhabitants. It is normal for a party of Jewish schoolchildren on an outing to be accompanied by an armed guard.

63

Continued hostilities create more homeless people all the time. This scene shows the makeshift Shatilla camp in Beirut, June 1985.

Of an estimated 4.5 million Palestinians today, just under 2 million are registered as refugees; many of these still draw UNRWA rations. About 600,000 – those living within Israel's 1948 borders – have some formal national rights, but their standard of living, education, and employment prospects are far inferior to their Jewish counterparts. Over 250,000 of the 1.3 million Palestinians living under Israeli military occupation in the West Bank and Gaza Strip are in refugee camps. For them, curfews, collective punishments, arbitrary arrest and imprisonment, demolition of homes, and school closures have become the norm. Seizure of land and water supplies for Israeli settlements has deprived the occupied Palestinians of much of the basis of agricultural subsistence, while Israel's economic domination has stifled local trade and industry. In Israeli-owned enterprises, many Palestinians receive half the wage of an

Israeli worker. Trade unions, like other political or nationalist organizations, are illegal. The skilled and educated inevitably see no future there and leave, although remaining in the area has become a central principle of Palestinian nationalism.

Some of the exiled Palestinians have adopted foreign nationality, particularly in Jordan, which hosts about one million of the refugees, but most suffer the stateless insecurity of a refugee existence. Ironically, the Palestinians have become the new "Jews" of the world. Like the Jews, they are high-achievers, and have seized upon education in particular as an escape route from oppression. Drawn by the oil boom opportunities of the 1960s and 1970s, many Palestinians moved to the Arab Gulf states, where some 500,000 live today. Through education, hard work and high motivation, many have amassed considerable wealth and, like the Jews who emigrated to America in the last century, have come to be resented for their success and clannishness.

The West Bank, 1984. Dheisheh refugee camp has been sealed off as a mark of collective punishment, whereby Palestinian refugees are all made to suffer for the guerrilla warfare conducted by a few.

In 1980, Bassam Shaka'a lost both legs in a car-bomb explosion for which members of the Jewish underground are now standing trial. Today, he is an influential force in the Palestinian struggle.

The war in Lebanon in 1982 completed the process of Palestinian disillusionment with the Arab governments, which began with the defeat of 1967. It also caused the long-standing ideological rift within the PLO to erupt into inter-Palestinian violence. Breakaway factions backed by Syria, opposed to Yasser Arafat's involvement with Jordan and Egypt and incensed by his flirtation with American-sponsored peace moves, battled against the last independent PLO stronghold in northern Lebanon. In December 1983, Arafat and his military supporters were evacuated from Tripoli by ship, a humiliating repeat of their departure from Beirut after the Israeli siege of 1982. Today the PLO is dispersed throughout the Arab world, and the refugees left behind in Lebanon are now caught up with the country's new political force, the Shi'ite Muslims.

13
The future ?

A military solution to the Palestine conflict now seems impossible. For Israel, endless warfare has divided its people, bankrupted its economy, and accelerated Jewish emigration, yet the country's security is as precarious as ever. Palestinian nationalism has not been crushed but invigorated and strengthened by oppression. Nevertheless, twenty years of armed struggle have not liberated a single inch of Palestine nor increased the prospect of an Israeli withdrawal from occupied territory.

The Gaza Strip, 1984. As Palestinians leave their homes in search of peace, Israeli settlement continues. This synagogue is being built in the shape of the Star of David.

Future generations are already involved in the conflict. This seven-year-old supporter of Yasser Arafat is armed with a machine gun.

The peace process has been a series of failures and missed opportunities, of which Camp David is the most striking example. After the 1973 war, both superpowers cooperated for a period in the search for a peace formula which reflected the new Arab–Israeli balance of power, but this unique chance was ruined by the bilateral agreement which in practice never touched on the Palestine issue. For Israel, Camp David quickly turned sour. Its Arab architect, President Sadat, was assassinated in October 1981, and although Egypt stuck to the treaty and regained occupied Sinai in

Cairo, October 1981. Egypt's President Mubarak with Israel's prime minister, Menachem Begin, at President Sadat's funeral.

April 1982, the invasion of Lebanon left Egyptian–Israeli relations broken once again. Sadat's successor, President Mubarak, has begun to return Egypt to the Arab fold, having already restored relations with Jordan.

There have been other peace initiatives since Camp David. In June 1980, the European Community members issued the Venice Declaration, which called for the full exercise of the Palestinian right to self-determination and for the PLO to be involved in any negotiations. In August 1981, Crown Prince Fahd of Saudi Arabia indicated Saudi willingness to recognize Israel in return for Israel's withdrawal from the occupied territories and the establishment there of an independent Palestinian state. These proposals were endorsed by the Palestine National Council in February 1983. In September 1982, President Reagan announced a plan for Palestinian self-government in the occupied territories "in association with Jordan." All ideas for returning the West Bank and Gaza Strip to Arab control were rejected outright by the Begin government in Israel, but today there is a new left–right coalition in power whose Labor leader,

Shimon Peres, leader of the coalition government in Israel, meets President Reagan. Peres is hopeful that a "territory for peace" may be possible in the Middle East.

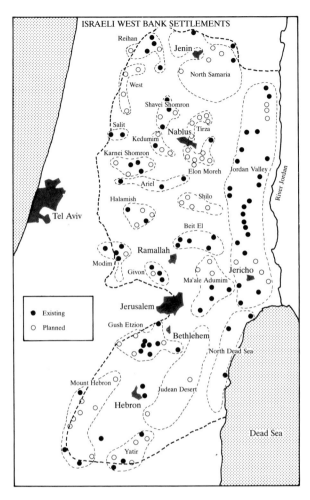

ISRAELI WEST BANK SETTLEMENTS

Reihan
Jenin
North Samaria
West
Shavei Shomron
Salit
Nablus
Tirza
Kedumim
Karnei Shomron
Elon Moreh
Jordan Valley
Halamish
Shilo
Tel Aviv
Beit El
Ramallah
Modim
Givon
Jericho
Ma'ale Adumim
● Existing
○ Planned
Jerusalem
Gush Etzion
Bethlehem
North Dead Sea
Mount Hebron
Judean Desert
Hebron
Dead Sea
Yatir

River Jordan

Although it is territory acquired through warfare, many consider the West Bank to be part of Israel. This map shows Israeli settlement blocs in existence in 1981 and ones planned for the future.

Shimon Peres, has shown interest in the idea of "territory for peace."

Central to this concept is the only peace formula accepted by most parties to the conflict, UN Resolution 242. (See page 73.) This is also the basis of the latest major peace initiative, the Jordanian–PLO accord of February 1985, which goes some way to meeting the Reagan Plan by proposing a Jordanian–Palestinian confederation in the occupied territories, but which also envisaged negotiations including the PLO and the members of the UN Security Council, one of which is the USSR. Israel and the US remain opposed, however, to involving either the USSR or the PLO in a settlement. The position the United States, whose unique influence over Israel makes it the key to any solution, is that the PLO must first explicitly accept Resolution 242, with its implied recognition and acceptance of Israel. For the PLO this represents a major difficulty because, alone among modern states, Israel has no internationally agreed frontiers.

The UN partition plan of 1947 envisaged a Jewish state in just over half of Palestine; the conquests of 1948 fixed its limits for the time at just over three-quarters of Palestine. Today most Israelis consider East Jerusalem, the West Bank, the Gaza Strip and the Golan Heights an integral part of Israel; some Israeli extremists even believe large parts of Egypt, Jordan, Syria, Iraq and Lebanon belong to Israel by right, as promised in the Bible. The Palestinians ask: which Israel are they to recognize. Blanket recognition, they argue, could well endorse their dispossession. Yasser Arafat has made it clear that recognition of Israel must be reciprocated by a recognition of Palestinian national rights. The result so far is a chicken-and-egg deadlock.

Meanwhile, the unresolved conflict grinds on. Syria, whose manipulation of the situation in Lebanon contributed

Amman, Jordan, 1983. Yasser Arafat and King Hussein, who once fought over Palestine rights in Jordan, now seek an agreement which will prevent war with Israel.

71

so much to Israel's empty-handed retreat from the country, is currently being armed on a large scale with the latest Soviet technology. Potentially the most dangerous conflict may be over the future of the occupied territories. There the ceaseless expansion of Israeli settlements is not only destroying any hope of a future Palestinian–Israeli formula for coexistence but threatening to displace the last major body of Palestinians from Palestine. If Israel were to provoke a mass exodus of Arabs from the West Bank into Jordan, this would almost certainly precipitate a major war. Fear of this provides the impetus behind the current efforts of King Hussein and Yasser Arafat to reach a settlement with Israel.

The prospect of further Arab–Israeli wars is a deeply ominous one for world peace as a whole. The polarization of the Middle East along East–West lines is far enough advanced for the possibility of superpower involvement and confrontation to be present at all times. Israel has also acquired its own nuclear weapons, and it cannot be long before at least one Arab state possesses them too. It may not be irrelevant to recall Biblical prophecy and remember that Armageddon is situated in what is today Israel.

Beirut, June 1985. Shi'ite guerrillas hijacked an American airliner and held its crew and passengers as hostages. They were released in return for Labanese prisoners detained by Israel.

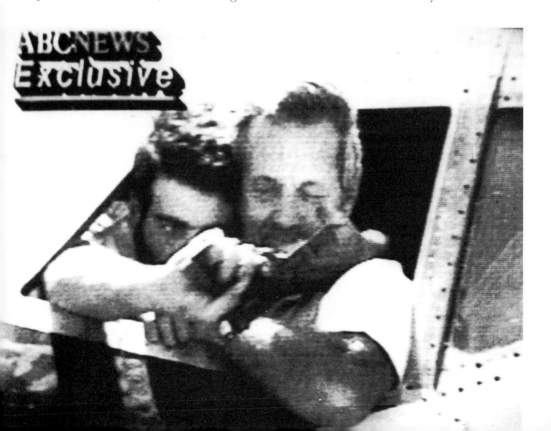

United Nations' Security Council Resolution on the Middle East (November 22, 1967)

THE SECURITY COUNCIL

Expressing its continuing concern with the grave situation in the Middle East,

Emphasizing the inadmissibility of the acquisition of territory by war and the need to work for a just and lasting peace in which every state in the area can live in security,

Emphasizing further that all member states in their acceptance of the Charter of the United Nations have undertaken a commitment to act in accordance with Article 2 of the Charter,

1. *Affirms* that the fulfillment of Charter principles requires the establishment of a just and lasting peace in the Middle East which should include the application of both the following principles:

(i)   Withdrawal of Israeli armed forces from territories of recent conflict;

(ii) Termination of all claims or states of belligerency and respect for and acknowledgment of the sovereignty, territorial integrity and political independence of every state in the area and their right to live in peace within secure and recognized boundaries free from threats or acts of force;

2. *Affirms further* the necessity

(a)   For guaranteeing freedom of navigation through international waterways in the area;

(b)   For achieving a just settlement of the refugee problem;

(c)   For guaranteeing the territorial inviolability and political independence of every state in the area, through measures including the establishment of demilitarized zones;

3. *Requests* the Secretary General to designate a special representative to proceed to the Middle East to establish and maintain contacts with the states concerned in order to promote agreement and assist efforts to achieve a peaceful and accepted settlement in accordance with the provisions and principles in this resolution.

4. *Requests* the Secretary General to report to the Security Council on the progress of the efforts of the special representative as soon as possible.

Glossary

Annexation   This occurs where one country takes possession of territory belonging to another.

Anti-Semitism   Semites are people speaking a semitic language (such as Aramaic, Ethiopic or, as some Jews do, Hebraic). Anti-Semitism is a hatred of Semites, resulting in the persecution of Jewish people through the ages.

"Arab awakening"   Arab reaction at the end of the nineteenth century against Turkish cultural domination. Under the rule of the Ottoman Empire, groups like the Palestinians felt the necessity for a return to the neglected religious and cultural aspects of Islam.

Arab Higher Committee   A group representing the various Arab parties, formed on April 25, 1936, to protect the interests of Palestinian Arabs threatened by Jewish hostilities and immigration.

Armageddon   The imagined final battleground of the struggle among all the nations, predicted in the Bible, which will bring about the end of the world, the Apocalypse.

Autonomy   The right of a state or country to self-government.

Colonization   The establishment of a group of people in a nation or area new to them, usually after evicting former inhabitants.

Economic sanction   Penalty or reward given to one country by another through measures taken to affect their economy, such as restricting trade or withdrawing loans.

Exodus   Mass emigration from a country or state, especially the Israelites from Egypt in 1300 B.C., and Jews fleeing from eastern European persecution in 1882.

Hagannah   A "secret army" trained by socialist Zionists from 1921 onward to enable Jews to establish and protect land ownership rights in Palestine. A forerunner of the Israeli Army, the Hagannah gradually moved from defensive to offensive actions in pursuance of this plan.

Holocaust   Huge slaughter of people, usually by burning. In particular the destruction of six million Jews by the Nazi government during World War II under orders from German dictator Adolf Hitler.

Ideology A body of ideas that form a coherent system, often linked to a political plan, or way of thinking, that affects social reform.

Imperialism The formation, acquisition, or maintenance of a large group of states known as an empire and controlled by one government or emperor. Traditionally it has involved the imposition of authority for exploitative and/or beneficial ends by the conquering country.

Islam The religion of Muslims who believe there is one God, revealed to the prophet Muhammad in A.D. 600.

Islamic fundamentalism Popular religious movement consisting of Muslim extremists prepared to use terrorist tactics to achieve political ends. In 1981 they assassinated President Sadat because they saw his treaty with Israel as a betrayal of the Palestinians.

Judaization Also known as de-Arabization. The obliteration of all traces of former Arab inhabitants from Palestine, for example by renaming villages.

League of Nations An international body, set up in 1919, to secure peace, justice, and international cooperation. It was superseded in 1954 by the United Nations.

Mandate Power conferred by the League of Nations whereby a developed nation can guide a nondeveloped one to independence.

PLO The Palestine Liberation Organization, founded in 1964, initially with the aim of creating a state for Palestinian Arabs and removing the state of Israel.

Polarization The movement in two contrary directions of related forces, objects, ideas, or groups of people.

Radical Favoring thorough constitutional, social, and political reform.

Shi'ite Muslims Members of an Islamic sect who recognize Ali, Muhammad's son-in-law, as his successor.

Sovereignty Supreme and independent power over an area.

Transjordan In 1923, the British granted independence to what was then called Transjordan, henceforth Jordan.

Turkish Ottoman Empire The Turkish Empire in Europe, Africa, and Asia, which lasted from the late thirteenth century until the end of World War I.

Venice Declaration Formal affirmation by the European Economic Community (EEC) in 1980 that its members favored the Palestinian right to self-determination of their future, and involvement in peace negotiations.

Index

Picture acknowledgments

The author and publishers acknowledge the loan of the following pictures for this book: Associated Press *cover*, 72; Camera Press Limited 54; Imperial War Museum 28; Middle East Centre, Oxford 15, 25, 38 (Jerusalem and East Mission Collection), 21 (Blyth Collection), 31 (American Colony Collection), 34 (Pollock Collection); The Photo Source 60; Popperfoto *frontispiece*; TOPHAM 8, 10, 11 (both), 12, 16, 22, 26, 29, 32, 41, 43, 44, 46, 47, 49, 50, 53, 59, 62, 68 (both), 69, 71; TORDAI 18, 36, 37, 48, 63, 65, 66, 67; United Nations Relief & Works Agency (UNRWA) 45, 51, 64; Wayland Picture Library 14, 20, 23, 57. The maps on pages 9, 13, 27, 30, 33, 35, 40, 42, 52, 56, 61 and 70 were drawn by Malcolm Walker.